How Organizations Learn

Investigate, Identify, Institutionalize

Also available from ASQ Quality Press:

Recognition, Gratitude, and Celebration
Patrick L. Townsend and Joan E. Gebhardt

Quality Makes Money: How to Involve Every Person on the Payroll in a Complete Quality Process (CQP)
Pat Townsend and Joan Gebhardt

Inside Knowledge: Rediscovering the Source of Performance Improvement
David Fearon & Steven A. Cavaleri

Everyday Excellence: Creating a Better Workplace through Attitude, Action, and Appreciation
Clive Shearer

Linking Customer and Employee Satisfaction to the Bottom Line
Derek Allen and Morris Wilburn

Leadership For Results: Removing Barriers to Success for People, Projects, and Processes
Tom Barker

Work Overload: Redesigning Jobs to Minimize Stress and Burnout
Frank M. Gryna

Making Change Work: Practical Tools for Overcoming Human Resistance to Change
Brien Palmer

The Team Effectiveness Survey Workbook
Robert W. Bauer and Sandra S. Bauer

Root Cause Analysis: Simplified Tools and Techniques, Second Edition
Bjørn Andersen and Tom Fagerhaug

The Certified Manager of Quality/Organizational Excellence Handbook: Third Edition
Russell T. Westcott, editor

Enabling Excellence: The Seven Elements Essential to Achieving Competitive Advantage
Timothy A. Pine

To request a complimentary catalog of ASQ Quality Press publications, call 800-248-1946, or visit our Web site at http://www.asq.org/quality-press.

How Organizations Learn

Investigate, Identify,
Institutionalize

Patrick L. Townsend and
Joan E. Gebhardt

ASQ Quality Press
Milwaukee, Wisconsin

American Society for Quality, Quality Press, Milwaukee, WI 53203
© 2008 by ASQ
All rights reserved. Published 2007.
Printed in the United States of America.

13 12 11 10 09 08 07   5 4 3 2 1

Library of Congress Cataloging-in-Publication Data

Townsend, Patrick L.
  How organizations learn : investigate, identify, institutionalize / Patrick L. Townsend and Joan E. Gebhardt.
    p. cm.
  Rev. ed. of: How organizations learn. 1999.
  Includes bibliographical references and index.
  ISBN-13: 978-0-87389-727-3
  1. Organizational learning. I. Gebhardt, Joan E. II. Title.
  HD58.82.T68 2007
  658.4'06--dc22
                              2007034569

Originally published 1999, Crisp Publications, Inc.

No part of this book may be reproduced in any form or by any means, electronic, mechanical, photocopying, recording, or otherwise, without the prior written permission of the publisher.

Publisher: William A. Tony
Acquisitions Editor: Matt T. Meinholz
Project Editor: Paul O'Mara
Production Administrator: Randall Benson

ASQ Mission: The American Society for Quality advances individual, organizational, and community excellence worldwide through learning, quality improvement, and knowledge exchange.

Attention Bookstores, Wholesalers, Schools, and Corporations: ASQ Quality Press books, videotapes, audiotapes, and software are available at quantity discounts with bulk purchases for business, educational, or instructional use. For information, please contact ASQ Quality Press at 800-248-1946, or write to ASQ Quality Press, P.O. Box 3005, Milwaukee, WI 53201-3005.

To place orders or to request a free copy of the ASQ Quality Press Publications Catalog, including ASQ membership information, call 800-248-1946. Visit our Web site at www.asq.org or http://www.asq.org/quality-press.

∞ Printed on acid-free paper

Quality Press
600 N. Plankinton Avenue
Milwaukee, Wisconsin 53203
Call toll free 800-248-1946
Fax 414-272-1734
www.asq.org
http://www.asq.org/quality-press
http://standardsgroup.asq.org
E-mail: authors@asq.org

Contents

Chapter 1 Jumping-Off Point for Learning 1
   Benchmarking the Three I's 3
   Defining the After-Action Review 4
   Parallels Between the Army and the
      Quality Movement 5
   Avoiding the Major Pitfall 5

**Chapter 2 Investigate and Identify:
          After-Action Reviews** 7
   The Birth of After-Action Reviews 9

Chapter 3 Spreading Leadership Skills 11
   A Shocking Discovery 12
   Cohesion Through Learning 14
   Link to Quality 15

**Chapter 4 Training the Indispensable
          Participant** 17
   Filling the Observer Controller Role 18
   The Art of Stepping Aside 19
   Disagreement Doesn't Have to
      Be Disagreeable 20
   Watch Those Details 22
   General Sullivan's Helpful Hints 23

Chapter 5   Getting to the Nitty-Gritty 25
Skeleton of an After-Action Review 26
Sharing a Vision 27
Data-Rich, but Not Data-Driven 28
Pick and Choose 30
No Fault, No Foul 31

Chapter 6   After-Action Reviews from a
Civilian Perspective 33
Facilitating Team Learning 34
Somewhere Over the Horizon 35
Benefits from an After-Action Review 36

Chapter 7   How the Army CALLs for Help 37
In War and in Peace 38
Do We Know That or Not? 40
Success and Failure 42
The CALL Experience 42
It Works! 44
Summing Up 45
If You Don't Already Do It, Start Now 45

Chapter 8   A New Learning Cycle 47
Jump-Start 49

Chapter 9   Taking AARs International 51
Converting the Wary 52
Giving It a Try 53
Assessing the Results 54

Chapter 10 Exploring the Depths of Knowledge ... 55
    Success from the Ground Down 56
    We Struck a Gusher! 58

Chapter 11 Choosing Success 61
    Investigate, Identify, Institutionalize 62

References 65

Further Reading 66

Index 67

About the Authors 71

1
Jumping-Off Point for Learning

Throughout the early 1960s, John Thomas of the United States and Valery Brumel of the Soviet Union set the standard for "world class" in the high jump. In Rome at the 1960 Olympics, Brumel tied another jumper at 7'1" and brought home the silver medal; pregame favorite Thomas finished third with a jump of 7' 1/4". Four hard-working years and less than an inch later, the 1964 contest was the crowning event of their long-running, two-man competition. At that Olympics held in Tokyo, they both jumped 7' 1 3/4", an Olympic record. Brumel took home the gold because he had fewer misses.

Then in 1968, Dick Fosbury arrived on the scene. He was the inventor of a radical approach to high jumping that became known as the Fosbury Flop, and his Olympic jump of 7' 4 1/4" in Mexico City was a quantum leap forward, a spectacular 2 1/2" increase (see Figure 1). The excitement he generated was enormous. For most television viewers, Fosbury appeared to come out of nowhere. Sports enthusiasts in Oregon, where he had been jumping in his own unorthodox manner for five years, first at Medford High, then at Oregon State, knew better.

Breakthrough improvements—whether a new idea or a new product—have a way of inspiring the publicity necessary for them to become commonplace. By the 1972 Olympics in Munich, thirteen of the sixteen high jump

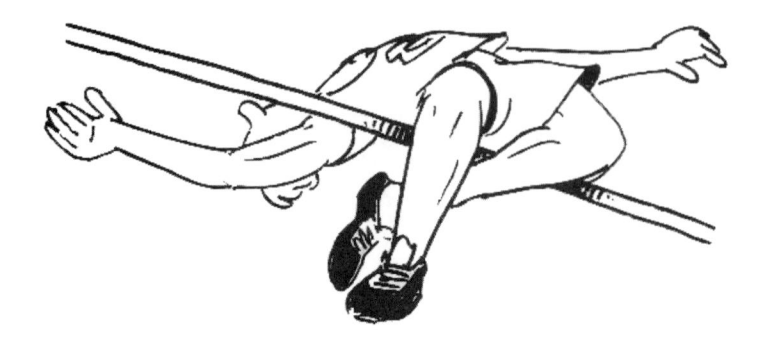

Figure 1 The Fosbury Flop.

competitors had adopted Fosbury's approach. Those who didn't, didn't win. Incremental improvements, on the other hand, have a more difficult time working their way into everyday activities. Usually, it's because no one knows about them. In the case of the Fosbury Flop, a visual demonstration of how to perform the flop was immediately available thanks to mass communication. As aspiring high jumpers tried the flop, they discovered that they, too, had higher jumps. But what if there had been no press coverage and no television in 1968? What if the only information was a line in the record books reading 7′ 4 1/4″? What then?

The Fosbury Flop story illustrates the three conditions necessary for effective learning to take place. First, high jumpers were seeking improvement; second, a successful new technique appeared; and third, high jumpers heard about it and tried it. Organizations also learn under the same conditions: people are actively looking, successful approaches are discovered, and the organization captures the knowledge and encourages everyone to try new things. This sequence can be associated with three words that together form a cycle of learning: *investigating* the situation is the first step; *identifying* failures and successes is the second; and availability of the information and willingness to use it, *institutionalizing* the lesson so that it becomes "the way things are done," is the third (see Figure 2). Only when the knowledge reaches the third stage does new behavior occur on a predictable basis—and only then is the stage set for the next improvement.

BENCHMARKING THE THREE I'S

This book examines this 3-I learning cycle—investigate, identify, institutionalize—as it takes place in the U.S. Army. Prominent companies such as General Electric, Motorola, Harley-Davidson, and Amoco have taken advantage of the army's experiences as they've moved through this cycle, reinventing themselves as learning organizations. These companies have gleaned valuable lessons from the army's After-Action Reviews (AARs) and the Center for Army Lessons Learned (CALL) in much the same way that

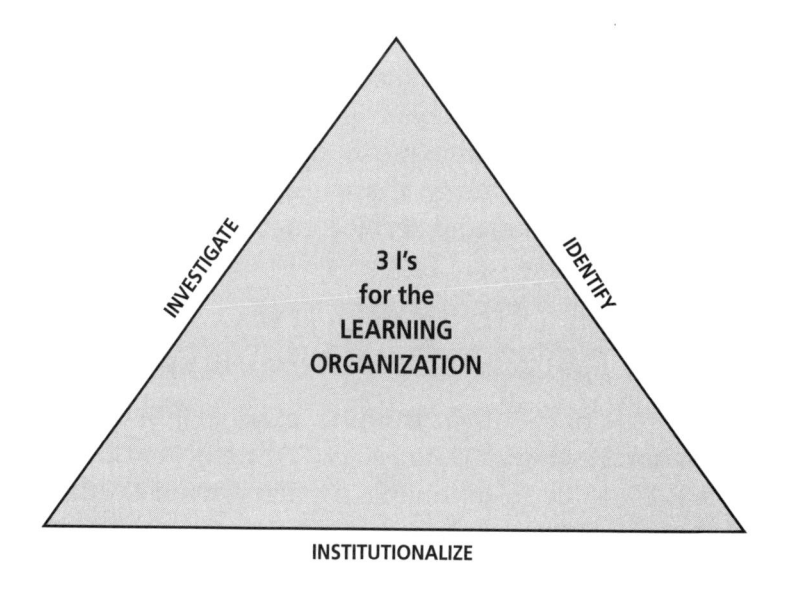

Figure 2 The Three "I" Words.

Malcolm Baldrige National Quality Award winner Xerox benefited from L.L. Bean's procedures for handling phone calls. The army offers these lessons as part of the Business Outreach Program sponsored by the Strategic Studies Institute at the Army War College, Carlisle Barracks, Pennsylvania. The army is also engaged in a cross-pollination of ideas with academe: Harvard Business School has developed a videotape on AARs, and the army has become a member of the Society for Organizational Learning at MIT.

The Baldrige Award also uses a 3-I approach to learning. Baldrige Award applications ask companies to describe how they handle quality issues. Preliminary judges evaluate the approaches and decide which companies merit a visit from a group of examiners, who inform a panel of nine judges of their findings. At that point, the judges identify what is worth emulating and designate winners. To be sure that valuable information receives the widest possible distribution, Award winners are pledged to teach others about those techniques they find useful in improving quality. The goal is to institutionalize best practices in corporate America. Although the investigative mechanism is essentially passive—companies must take the initiative either to apply for the award or to query Baldrige Award winners—several valuable tools have been institutionalized since the Award's inception in 1988. Among these tools are benchmarking, partnering, Six Sigma, and service guarantees.

DEFINING THE AFTER-ACTION REVIEW

According to the Army's training manual FM 100-25, an After-Action Review is defined as: "A method of providing feedback to units by involving participants in the training diagnostics process in order to increase and reinforce training. An After-Action Review is a professional discussion of an event, focused on performance standards, that enables the trainees to discover for themselves what happened, why it happened, and how to sustain strengths and improve weaknesses in performance."

PARALLELS BETWEEN THE ARMY AND THE QUALITY MOVEMENT

Wherever appropriate, parallels will be drawn in this book between the army's experience and the quality movement. The assumption that everything can be improved is one of the many features that the army's combination of AARs and CALL shares with quality. Another commonality is the emphasis on integrating working and learning, each supporting the other. Work, assessed via an AAR or quality team or suggestion system, leads to identification of possibilities for improvement. Information analyzed identifies desired procedures. Institutionalization creates new data, and the cycle begins again.

AVOIDING THE MAJOR PITFALL

With both the army's approach and the Baldrige Award, the trickiest part of the learning cycle is the willingness of organizations to adapt useful information after it is available. The president of Paul Revere Insurance Group, Aubrey K. Reid, Jr., articulated the problem in 1984. His company was one of the front-runners in the quality revolution in the United States. As word of its success spread—the first notable success by a paper-and-ideas organization—other insurance companies came to call. Visitors to the company were amazed to find that very little information about its quality effort was proprietary. At the end of a day of touring and briefings, an official from another insurance firm asked Reid why he was so open with potential competitors. Reid said, "First of all, we learn from your questions. Second, when you go back to your own company, you'll most likely put aside what you learn here because of day-to-day pressures. Third, if you actually do imitate us, we've got a big head start, and we're not going to slow down."

In a similar vein, the U.S. Army welcomes the leaders of military forces from countries all over the world to take a look at its training methods. Those methods, the centerpiece of the army's journey from Vietnam to the Gulf War and beyond, are not arcane; however, few, if any, will make a serious commitment of people, time, and resources to copy what they see. Although a combination of AARs and CALL are relatively straightforward and easy to understand, they are difficult to implement fully. But, as with quality, the results justify the effort.

2
Investigate and Identify: After-Action Reviews

One spring day in 1997, a platoon of scouts, part of a division of troops from Washington state training at Ft. Irwin, California, the army's desert training center, were clustered around a jeep, waiting to begin an AAR. On the running board sat an observer controller (OC). To one side stood the young lieutenant in command of the platoon. The division had just completed its first training exercise of its month-long visit and had been beaten badly by the opposing force. The scouts had been particularly hard-hit. Laser sensors on their uniforms and equipment indicated that the entire platoon had been either "killed" or "wounded" the night before.

To open the proceedings, the OC appointed a volunteer to take notes, then asked conversationally, "What's the rule?"

"No hurt feelings!" the troops responded vigorously, and the AAR began (see Figure 3).

No hurt feelings? In the army? It was advice that participants in this particular AAR would need before the review was over. The platoon was called to task for neglecting to top off ammunition, water, and fuel supplies whenever it encountered friendly forces. ("What are we?" "Scouts!" "What do scouts do?" "Scrounge!") The lieutenant's failure to delegate became the vehicle for a short lesson on leadership. ("Does that mean you have to do it all yourself? No, everyone needs to know how to read those graphic

Figure 3 Words to live by.

symbols so they'll pay more attention. You just have to see that the job gets done. And then you have time to do what only you can do.")

Pocket-notebook-size operations manual in hand ("Take a note—we need an index in this thing…"), participants deconstructed events of the previous sixteen hours. Nothing was too mundane, nothing too sensitive to analyze. One of the thornier questions asked was why a second jeep was ordered to a location where a first jeep had been ambushed, only to be "destroyed." Someone ventured a guess that there might be some strategic consideration of which the platoon was unaware. The lieutenant promised to carry the question to the AAR at the next level of command. It was a typical AAR.

THE BIRTH OF AFTER-ACTION REVIEWS

AARs, the first link in the army's chain of learning, are a post-Vietnam War addition to the way the army does things. They grew out of the army's frustration at being involved in what was essentially a losing effort. The army looked for ways to ensure that the loss would not be repeated, and AARs offered part of the answer. In the words of a standard briefing given at the national training center in Ft. Irwin:

> *An After-Action Review is a professional discussion of an event, focused on performance standards, that enables soldiers to discover for themselves what happened, why it happened, and how to sustain strengths and improve on weaknesses. It is a tool leaders and units can use to get maximum benefit from every mission or task. It provides:*
>
> - *Candid insights into specific soldier, leader, and unit strengths and weaknesses from various perspectives*
>
> - *Feedback and insight critical to battle-focused training*
>
> - *Details often lacking in evaluation reports alone*

In other words, the AAR provides a forum for participants to investigate a situation, and a problem-solving process designed to help individuals and units identify strengths and weaknesses, propose solutions, and adopt a course of action to assure effective behavior in the future. Because everyone knows that an AAR will follow an activity, people are actively looking at what works and what does not. Once lessons are identified, they are passed on to a common database for possible use by other units. An AAR also provides a reliable way for people at the working end of the chain of command to exchange information with those at the top.

A succinct appraisal of the impact of AARs is offered by a former army chief of staff, the service's senior four-star general, General Gordon H. Sullivan, in his book *Hope Is Not a Method:* "For America's army, the AAR was the key to turning the corner and institutionalizing organizational learning." Sullivan's comments on AARs have a special credibility because he and his staff conducted AARs to assess his and their actions while he was chief of staff. As with virtually every management and leadership tool, example remains the surest teaching technique. The news that Sullivan himself was involved in AARs spread via the army communications grapevine and helped to institutionalize the practice throughout the army. He admits that the sessions were often uncomfortable, but he asserts that they not only helped him to improve what he did, but also strengthened his relationship with his staff and helped them to better understand how they could support him.

Now more than twenty years old, the AAR has itself gone through an investigate–identify–institutionalize cycle in the U.S. Army. A sure sign that it has been institutionalized is its use as a verb by young army enlisted personnel who commonly refer to having "AAR'd" some problem or another. To conduct an AAR, all an organization has to do is adopt the ground rules and adapt the procedures, both of which are explained in the following chapters.

3
Spreading Leadership Skills

As it backed out of Vietnam in the mid-1970s, the U.S. Army decided that at least one thing was wrong with its past habits: it needed to broaden its leadership base. In a world in which everything was moving faster and enemies could deliver their ordnance over greater and greater distances, there would be no time in the future to leave preparations solely in the hands of the generals. Soldiers of every rank would need to develop analytical and communication skills or the army would squander brain power, an experience that it—and the United States—could not afford.

The example has obvious parallels in the business world. When information and people move more rapidly than ever imagined less than a decade ago and competitors easily deliver products to market anywhere on the planet, the need for effective independent action becomes critical and the idea of restricting thinking to one small group of seniors managers is ludicrous.

An excellent definition of leadership is that it creates the environment in which others can self-actualize in the process of completing the task. In short, good leaders develop other leaders. That definition also comes close to being a working description of the mechanics and objectives of an AAR. An AAR assumes skilled leadership at every level, both from the point of view that AARs provide an environment in which everyone is expected to contribute and from the point of view that AARs are conducted by units at every point on the organizational diagram.

A SHOCKING DISCOVERY

In 1995, General Electric approached the army about setting up a two-and-a-half-day training session for a group of about forty senior and mid-level managers as part of its Executive Development Program. The group spent one day at Gettysburg Battlefield talking strategy and a day and a half in a seminar on leadership. Two weeks later, they went to Ft. Irwin to observe an AAR. What impressed the executives was the openness of the exchange between the ranks. No one forgot his or her position, but a private first class felt perfectly free to say to a general, "Sir, that order did make my job more difficult." Translation: I'd like an explanation. And the general would respond. Polite disputation is not only allowed at an AAR, it is expected. In the videotape on the AAR produced by the Harvard Business School, one young army officer went so far as to characterize withholding valid criticism as a "career-threatening" move.

Clearly, an AAR challenges the self-confidence of anyone who forgets the "no hurt feelings" admonition and takes as a personal affront any suggestions to improve anything that falls under his or her auspices. Senior army officers had to make a conscious decision to admit that they didn't have all the answers and that the men and women at all levels of the army knew things that they didn't. In an AAR, people learn from the knowledge of others (see Figure 4).

Senior managers of a business organization will also have to deliberately surrender their stranglehold on the flow of the information and ideas. The military does, admittedly, have some advantages over the average civilian organization when it comes to sharing information. Because of the mobility of personnel and the overriding altruistic mission of the military, it is easier for individuals to surrender to the common pool of knowledge information that would mark them as solitary (and, thus, valuable) experts in other organizations. For too many in the corporate world, the idea that knowledge is power leads to the pernicious belief that sharing knowledge means a diminution of power. This approach places the individual good ahead of the good of the organization and blocks possibly valuable information from being added to the corporate memory.

Figure 4   "I didn't know you knew that."

COHESION THROUGH LEARNING

Attendees at AARs function as peers, adults training adults, with everyone contributing a piece of the puzzle and helping to move the organization one step closer to achieving its highest potential. All attendees need to share the belief that the communication flow will be open, that the focus will be on performance rather than motivation, and that everyone's opinion, memories, and ideas will be welcomed. Only when this environment is established and maintained will everyone honestly discuss what they believe happened in sufficient detail and clarity so that not only will everyone understand what did and did not occur, but also why.

When soldiers and leaders actively participate to discover what happened and why, the AAR adheres to the best in educational and psychological research and thinking. Active participation greatly increases the amount of information retained. Direct involvement in discussions also increases an individual's motivation to accept the agreed-to lessons and change personal behavior in the future, even if that means admitting to errors in the past. Coupled with a mechanism for recording and disseminating mutually understood lessons (rather than relying on the pious hope that "we all learned something from this"), the odds of changes in behavior beneficial to the organization rise exponentially. If efforts to identify lessons and to inform appropriate people about the lessons are diligent, the institutionalization of lessons becomes less difficult, setting the stage for further improvements. Furthermore, establishing an atmosphere in which missteps are thought of as beginning points allows everyone to reexamine action and ideas. No one need settle for "good enough" when there is no penalty for looking again.

After observing several AARs at a national training center, one executive from Ford Motor Company concluded, "The army has scab-pickers par excellence." This would please Paul Allaire, the CEO of Baldrige-winner Xerox, who pointed out recently that U.S. companies would be well advised to shift from standard Western thinking, which advises, "If it ain't broke, don't fix it," to the Eastern philosophy of, "If it's not perfect, make it better." Regardless of how good things appear to be at a particular moment, the army believes that there is always room for improvement.

As the *AAR Guidebook* makes clear, "By involving appropriate commanders, staff, and troops in a professional discussion of 'How can we do better?,' the cohesiveness of the unit and the chain of command are simultaneously reinforced." A major benefit is the positive effect on morale. Using AARs, the army has built better teams by building better soldiers, one individual at a time, with the result that even though members of the teams change frequently, the organization retains the benefits. That is why the army of 1990 that went to Saudi Arabia was so much better than the army of 1975—even after a turnover of several hundred percent.

LINK TO QUALITY

The AAR represents a major improvement over traditional military after-action briefings. The difference is akin to the difference between staff meetings and quality team meetings. Even if the people at the two meetings are precisely the same, staff meetings tend to deal with yesterday plus a bit of today—and peek at tomorrow. A well-run quality meeting focuses on tomorrow and how to make it better by learning from today's lesson. In both an

AAR and a well-run quality meeting, the intent is to define measurable action and the assumption is that anything can be improved.

An AAR clone can serve as the centerpiece of any well-organized and well-directed quality process with its focus locked onto how to make things better in the future, as long as the organization pays attention to the idea of developing leaders at every level. As with a successful AAR, quality depends on good leadership. Changing the culture to accept leadership at every level is a daunting challenge. There is really no way to broaden the leadership base part way, to invest only a little time and effort, and have a reasonable hope for success. A hop of hope simply won't suffice; a leap of faith is required. Fortunately, civilian organizations can make a fact-based leap and build on the army's success.

4

Training the Indispensable Participant

"After-action reviews have become part of the army culture," said Brigadier General William S. Wallace, commanding general of the national training center at Ft. Irwin. "You'll find units all over the army that are using AARs to learn from their experience regardless of whether they are combat stations or home units. The advantage, however, of coming to a training center is that you have detached observers helping you because, frankly, you are rarely as honest with yourself as you might be unless someone is watching over you and keeping track."

Although it may be an advantage to have a trained Observer Controller present, it is not always possible. The army recognizes this, and when a trained OC is not available, the role is filled by the senior person present, often the commanding officer of the unit. The person acting as OC has the responsibility to ensure that the AAR is conducted in a participative manner, drawing out observations and opinions from all present. An OC keeps the discussion focused on the goal of determining what happened compared to what was expected or planned, and how to learn from the difference between the two. AARs are more productive when the OC is technically expert in the area being explored by the AAR, and whenever possible, he or she should be of at least equal rank to the senior person in the unit undertaking the AAR.

FILLING THE OBSERVER CONTROLLER ROLE

Whomever a civilian organization picks to fill the role of OC will be an early (and accurate) indicator of how serious senior management is about their attempt to replicate the army's success with the AAR. OCs must be, and must be believed to be, talented, knowledgeable people on their way up in the organization. When a unit makes a sacrifice for a person to become an OC for either a long- or short-term assignment, it is graphic proof that the project is important. Anything less and the word will be out that senior managers have chosen to talk in one direction and walk in another.

Developing OCs requires planning. Will the position of OC be a full-time job? If so, the organization will have to staff the position carefully. Will select people conduct AARs on a part-time basis? Will they be granted sufficient time to prepare for upcoming AARs? Where will the organization turn for training? Who besides OCs will educate employees at all levels about AARs? If people don't know in advance what an AAR is, what the intent is, and how the results will be used, any attempts at an AAR will most likely fall on hard times. If, for instance, people believe that the data being gathered are to be used as a weapon, an AAR could turn into a debacle and undermine future efforts.

Because of the importance of the OC, particularly early on, organizations need to spend the time and money necessary to make sure that the OC is ready and that he or she knows how to run the AAR, knows the business at hand, and will ask both "Did we do the right things?" and "Did we do things right?" types of questions—even when he or she already knows the "objective" answer. Given the technical knowledge of the OC, no doubt it will sometimes be difficult for the OC to hold back and not just present—in a lecture format—the answer that the OC thinks is "right."

THE ART OF STEPPING ASIDE

OCs must keep in mind the following admonition (from an instruction sheet on AARs given to college ROTC cadets undergoing summer training): "An AAR is not a critique. The facilitator will not simply recount his/her own assessment of the things the team did well or did poorly." Only by soliciting the opinions, memories, and insights of participants from a variety of levels and backgrounds can a clearer and more complete picture of what actually happened emerge. The OC's technical knowledge does, however, help him or her frame the best questions to move the discussion along without rendering judgments, and it helps the OC to assist participants in articulating the lessons they agree should be the basis for future action.

AARs are designed to be a pragmatic exercise that requires a common understanding of the end commitment to overall organizational excellence. If there is to be any hope of the AAR having a consistent and positive impact, diligent efforts at communication and education must begin long before the event that triggers a specific AAR so that the AAR can fit into the organizational context.

Although thoroughly participative and, in many ways, reflective of many of the management practices considered by old-line, authoritarian managers to be "New Age," the AAR is not a "feel-good" exercise. AARs are hard work, and no matter how impersonal the conversations or how focused everyone stays on the process and not the individual, some people may feel discouraged, particularly if it becomes clear in an AAR that they did not serve their comrades well.

To mitigate this effect, the OC needs to maintain a firm but gentle hand on the proceedings. While encouraging maximum participation, he or she must ensure that the discussion doesn't degenerate into a random, finger-pointing confrontation. A clear agenda combined with technical knowledge and the informed commitment of all participants helps them to identify both the positive and the negative and to focus on future possibilities.

Questions such as "What happened?" "Why did it happen?" "What was supposed to happen?" and "What can we learn?" serve as the catalysts for a stream of ideas. Overall, according to the OC's bible, *A Leader's Guide to After-Action Reviews* (see Figure 5), a discussion leader sets the tone by following a few simple rules:

- Enter the discussion only when necessary
- Reinforce the fact that it is permissible to disagree
- Focus on learning and encourage people to give honest opinions
- Use open-ended and leading questions to guide the discussion of soldier, leader, and unit performance

The *AAR Guidebook* goes so far to say that, "Except for making periodic summaries, the AAR leader rarely makes a declarative statement."

DISAGREEMENT DOESN'T HAVE TO BE DISAGREEABLE

The best way to reinforce the fact that it is permissible to disagree is to reemphasize two points that all participants are strongly encouraged to accept: no egos and no hurt feelings. As in the example in Chapter 2, OCs remind participants at the beginning of an AAR to leave their personal problems and thin skin at home. An essential ingredient of a successful AAR is tact. An AAR is not a case of "pure democracy" in action. No one forgets completely who he or she is or who anyone else is. Indeed, one of the OC's many responsibilities is to ensure that respect is maintained throughout the AAR: respect for the process, for the truth, and for each other. The willingness to risk one's personal security does not come naturally for most people. The only way to get there is by repeated examples that, over time, combine to assure people that the hips and the lips of the senior leadership are going in the same direction. By exercising tact, an OC models the behavior he or she

Figure 5 The observer controller's bible.

expects. In line with this, General Sullivan recommends that commanding officers use careful phrasing when conducting an AAR—asking, "What did you think I wanted you to do?" for example, rather than, "How did you manage to screw that up so thoroughly?"

WATCH THOSE DETAILS

The OC—or whoever is going to conduct the AAR—has myriad duties. The army's attention to detail is reflected in its admonition to OCs to consider how comfortable the seating will be for participants when picking a location for an AAR. If at all possible, no one should be distracted from the task at hand because he or she can't see what is going on or because a particular part of the participant's anatomy is suffering from spasms.

In addition to picking and preparing the meeting place, an OC must spend time in advance reviewing appropriate doctrine, deciding who should attend the AAR, choosing the quickest possible time that the AAR can be productively held, preparing training aids (to include articulating the mission or any other starting place that needs to be agreed to before any conversation about possible improvements can be fruitful), and observing key events. Depending on the level of the unit undertaking the AAR, the OC may have to seek out information from other AARs conducted by lower units, as well as archival information about how others have achieved the specified or similar missions.

GENERAL SULLIVAN'S HELPFUL HINTS

In his book *Hope Is Not a Method*, General Sullivan offers the following suggestions for conducting an AAR:

1. Do not start your AAR experience with an enormous, complex task; build the skills with simple but not inconsequential tasks.

2. Make sure you have as much information as possible about what really happened, and make sure every participant has access to that information as you go through the process.

3. Ensure that the leaders endorse the ground rules.

4. Finally, set aside enough time to really get into things. If you are reviewing a major project at a critical milestone with twenty or thirty members, it could easily take an afternoon to work through the important issues. If you don't allow enough time, you will be unlikely to get beyond the "measurables" and into the "unmeasurables," where the most significant learning can take place.

An effective OC blends technique with an understanding of the component parts of an AAR. Without both, an AAR can never reach its full potential.

5
Getting to the Nitty-Gritty

As presented in the previous chapters, AARs are based on a clear philosophy summed up by *A Leader's Guide to After-Action Reviews:*

- An AAR is a dynamic, candid, professional discussion of training that focuses on unit performance against the army standard for the task being trained. Everyone can, and should, participate if they have an insight, observation, or question which will help the unit identify and correct deficiencies or maintain strengths.

- An AAR is not a critique. No one, regardless of rank, position, or strength of personality, has all of the information or answers. After-Action Reviews maximize training benefits by allowing soldiers, regardless of rank, to learn from each other.

- An AAR does not grade success or failure. There are always weaknesses to improve and strengths to sustain.

It cannot be stated too often that AARs are not designed—and should not be used—to place blame. For one thing, events don't always go badly. The idea that AARs seek to enable learning from both successes and failures is an important one. At the human-nature level, the simple fact that the participants do not have to automatically assume that every AAR will be a painful exercise in *mea culpa* helps to maintain individual commitment. Often, an AAR is conducted after a successful experience, with an eye towards preserving that performance for the future.

SKELETON OF AN AFTER-ACTION REVIEW

According to *A Leader's Guide*, AARs have several "key points":

- They occur during or immediately after each event.
- They focus on intended training objectives.
- They focus on soldier, leader, and unit performance.
- They involve all participants in the discussion.
- They use open-ended questions.
- They relate to specific standards.
- They determine strengths and weaknesses.
- They link performance to subsequent training.

A Leader's Guide also provides a format, a sequence of events to be followed with the prompting of an OC:

1. Introduction and rules
2. Commander's mission and intent (what was supposed to happen)
3. Opposing force (OPFOR [read: competitor]) commander's mission and intent (when appropriate)
4. Relevant doctrine and tactics, techniques, and procedure (TTPs)
5. Summary of recent events (what happened)

6. Discussion of key issues (why it happened and how to improve)
7. Discussion of optional issues
8. Discussion of force protection issues (discussed throughout)
9. Closing comments (summary)

SHARING A VISION

The introduction and rules are covered in the philosophy of an AAR. The next step is to understand the mission so that everyone shares a common understanding of the desired outcome of their activity. Whether in the military or the civilian world, that discussion alone is highly valuable and, in many organizations, unusual. In its absence, people assume that others see their unit's job the same way they do, even though there has been no specific commentary on this subject. In one of the businesses that was highly successful in the early years of the U.S. quality revolution, one of the exercises that senior managers were required to do was to describe their department's function in just two words: one verb and one noun. (For instance, the function of the cafeteria was to "feed people.") Again and again, people who had been working together for years got into drawn-out, sometimes loud, arguments about how to describe what they did.

Members of an organization—and the members of each team within that organization—need to articulate what they think they currently do and what goal is currently being pursued. Unless they agree on the intellectual content, the standard against which they are measuring themselves and their results (that is, where they are today), and the standard for which they are reaching (that is, where they agree they want to be in the near future), definitive action is an illusion. It is impossible to measure the distance from

X to Y or to determine how to get from X to Y unless everyone agrees where X is and where Y is.

DATA-RICH, BUT NOT DATA-DRIVEN

The U.S. Army national training centers have huge collections of data available for use in an AAR: audiotapes of radio communications during training exercises, videotapes of specific events, electronic tracking of the locations of virtually all units at every minute of the event, and verbal reports by a variety of observers. Data, however, is only as good as the presentation that accompanies it. The OC is responsible for seeing that hard, factually irrefutable data enriches an AAR discussion but does not dictate solutions.

A Leader's Guide specifically warns against the gathering or use of "statistics for statistics' sake." As in a quality process, there are only two pertinent reasons for taking measurements (see Figure 6). The first is to generate new ideas and the second is to chart progress. If the charting indicates that progress is not what was hoped, then it is back to the first reason: to generate new ideas. If an organization—whether military or civilian, manufacturing or service, public or private—uses measurements primarily as a source of punishment, it will soon be plagued by institutionalized falsification of data (sometimes referred to simply as lying), and the rate of improvement of the organization will slow dramatically, if not stop entirely.

Data is used, however, to fulfill two of Sullivan's criteria in "Elements of the After-Action Review": "identifiable event, with associated standards" and "knowledge of what happened (ground truth)." Data also helps participants decide on future action. The *AAR Guidebook* states: "(a) No matter what the situation may be, alternative courses of action exist, and (b) leaders and soldiers should select from among these alternatives after evaluating what the probable consequences of each would be." Data helps with that evaluation.

According to the *Leader's Guide,* AARs are the dynamic link between task performance and execution to standard. The sense of urgency is maintained because standards change. In both civilian and military arenas, competitors are forever raising the bar. The emphasis on future behavior is the reason why AARs are not used to grade past behavior. Performance is measured and discussed but the focus is squarely on continually improving soldier and unit performance. By the end of an AAR, all participants must clearly understand what was good, bad, or average about their performance, so that they can move forward.

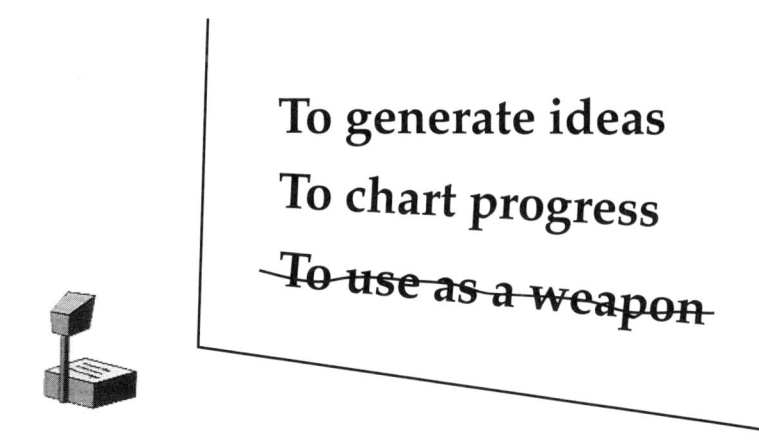

To generate ideas

To chart progress

~~To use as a weapon~~

Figure 6   Philosophy of measurement.

PICK AND CHOOSE

The *Leaders' Guide* presents two possible approaches for structuring the sequence of an AAR: chronological or by key event. The AAR can either step through what happened minute by minute or focus on particular episodes. The choice will be the OC's at the outset and will depend on his or her experience (both with AARs in general and with the specific unit in particular), the objective of the actions under discussion, and how, at the first glance, they played out.

The same source states that not all AARs are formal:

> *All AARs follow the same general format, involve the exchange of ideas and observations, and focus on improving training proficiency. How leaders conduct a particular AAR determines whether it is formal or informal. A formal AAR is resource intensive and involves the planning, coordination, and preparation of supporting training aids, the AAR site, and support personnel. Informal AARs require less preparation and planning.*

A less wordy way to differentiate between formal and informal AARs is provided by a chart on "training aids" in the same manual. Under the category "formal AARs," "video camera and monitor" and "terrain model" are among the options listed. Under the category "informal AARs, " one of the possibilities is "rocks and twigs." While an overall action that will lead to a formal, planned AAR is in progress, the OC may initiate a number of informal AARs, which require far less preparation and can be centered on one specific event. Often only a pad of paper or some kind of writing surface and a few leading questions are required to conduct an informal AAR.

Informal AARs have the obvious strength of "providing immediate feedback while the training is still fresh in soldiers' minds," but the army guidance calls for quick action at all levels. In the instance of a large-scale training exercise, AARs at the lower levels are required to take place within as little as an hour after the end of the action, while higher-level AARs have a "within six hours" requirement, a sequence that allows information about the view "from the bottom" to be included in the top-level AARs. The idea is that the fresher the memory, the more likely that the discussion will uncover points for improvement or preservation and the more likely that both will be internalized by the individuals and organization.

An organization needs both formal and informal AARs. Without formal AARs, informal ones will dry up and go away because, as with every management technique, if there is no obvious involvement and commitment by senior managers—to include the investment of their own time and ideas—enthusiasm at the lower levels will languish. Without informal AARs, formal ones will be data-starved and idea-starved.

NO FAULT, NO FOUL

Thousands of AARs, both formal and informal, are conducted at the army's national training centers. In addition to the training center at Ft. Irwin, there are two other "muddy boots" training centers, the Joint Readiness Training Center in Ft. Polk, Louisiana, and the Combat Maneuver Training Center in Hohenfels, Germany. In keeping with the spirit of continuously seeking improvement and not dwelling on the past, no permanent unit-specific records, scores, or evaluations are kept at the centers themselves. When a unit concludes its training and returns to its home base, all the data accumulated leaves with it. This allows the unit to continue to draw from the lessons learned while undergoing the training—and not to feel as though Big Brother back at headquarters is picking apart its track record.

The military (or any organization) has an abundance of methods for measuring, judging, and grading people without using data from an AAR. An AAR is not a replacement for those management efforts; rather, it is a marvelously effective addition to any organization's management practices, one that not only provides a bridge between methodologies, but also provides a way to improve them.

6
After-Action Reviews from a Civilian Perspective

Done well, AARs set an organization up for a series of victories and successes (large and small) and the possibility of making improvement a corporate habit. In fact, getting away from one-sided, top-down critiques and, instead, instituting group discussions mirrors the best of the quality movement.

One way for a business to begin AARs is to use the application for the Baldrige Award as the standard against which to compare current practices. With the Baldrige Award criteria as the "where we want to be" component and current behavior and results as the "where we are" component, the stage would be set for a series of AARs, perhaps as many as one per category (there are seven) and one per bureaucratic level in the organization, with the lower-level AARs taking place first. Such a plan might call for a network of OCs who could coordinate the information as it moves up the ladder. Such a bold enterprise would require thinking of previous performance as a blame-free "training session" conducted as preparation for the company of tomorrow.

On a less ambitious scale, an organization could conduct an AAR (or series of AARs) on a single topic, such as leadership. The key would still be to focus on yesterday and today to get to tomorrow. The impact of the use of measurements depends on the attitude of those extracting and using the data.

FACILITATING TEAM LEARNING

In an unpublished paper titled "Facilitating Team Learning: The After-Action Review," Philip Holland, of the Center for Executive Development in Cambridge, Massachusetts, and Lloyd Baird, of the School of Management of Boston University, provide a useful summary of what constitutes a successful AAR:

1. A review of the *intent* of the recent action

2. A reconstruction of whether that intent was achieved and key events, or *what happened*

3. A discussion of *lessons learned* from the action

4. Definition of *action implications* of the lessons learned

5. *Action,* based on the lessons learned

6. Sharing of those lessons with others

The first three steps constitute a particularly well-conducted review, something that may not be routine in every organization but is, at least, not uncommon. The last three steps make the whole process much more powerful: The stress is on the practical, and the emphasis is on the future, both the immediate future of the unit conducting the AAR and the long-range future of the organization as a whole.

In the same paper, Holland and Baird spell out guidelines for running an AAR, which are paraphrased below:

- *Who:* all those closest to the action, regardless of level

- *What:* not necessarily everything; do those with most potential for improvement

- *When:* as soon as possible after the event, when memories are fresh—when the team's intended purpose has or has not been met, or at some important milestone

- *Where:* virtually anywhere that doesn't impede discussion

- *Why:* to promote learning while the experience is fresh and, most important, to lead quickly to improved action

- *How long:* brief, usually under an hour but lasting as long as it takes

SOMEWHERE OVER THE HORIZON

According to Holland and Baird, an AAR should have three horizons—short-term, mid-term, and long-term. One of the real tricks to a successful AAR is maintaining focus on all three simultaneously because "short-term actions produce quick wins and further learning, while mid-term and long-term actions promote fundamental change."

The idea is to have an eye on the future while not being exclusively farsighted. To become the best at what you do in the long term, you must invest time and effort in the short term. By incorporating "What did we learn?" sessions into the normal evolution of specific chains of events, senior management sends a clear signal that improvement is high on the list of priorities. As noted previously, although the mechanics differ, the AAR process echoes what is best about a well-implemented quality process.

BENEFITS FROM AN AFTER-ACTION REVIEW

In addition to promoting continuous improvement by learning from experience, Holland and Baird see four other benefits to organizations using AARs, provided with paraphrased comments below:

- *Structured, purposeful dialogue* (by providing an agenda and a framework for leading participants through discussions and ensuring that they don't overlook possible areas for investigation).

- *Breaking hierarchical barriers* (by promoting an atmosphere in which what is said is more important than who said it). Admittedly, no process can absolutely guarantee a mindset that values everyone's input, but this at least has that mindset as a goal.

- *Reflection close to action* (by establishing the first attempt at reviewing what happened and drawing lessons from it on the spot, by the people who actually saw and did it). Anticipating the AAR encourages people to make mental and written notes about questions and ideas because they know that they'll get a chance to talk about them.

- *Recorded lessons* (by requiring that lessons be written down). An AAR enables participants to articulate ideas. Going from "Oh, yeah, we all think alike on that one" to "Here, written down, is what we agree is the lesson to be learned" creates lessons that are easier to remember and much, much easier to refer to later. If the goal is to share the lessons with other people, it is essential they be written.

7
How the Army CALLs for Help

In 1990, when the U.S.-led United Nations coalition moved into the Saudi Arabian desert, U.S. tanks began having severe operating problems. Filters for the tanks did not stop the "ingestion of dust." Simply put, motors stalled. It soon became apparent that the sand in the Saudi Arabian desert had a different consistency than sand found in the United States (see Figure 7). Looking for a solution, the army depended on AARs by army units in the desert, efforts by manufacturers' representatives on the scene, and coordination by members of CAATs (Collection and Analysis Teams), active duty personnel assigned by CALL (Center for Army Lessons Learned).

The CAATs' first task was to make partial and possible solutions from AARs available to every unit working on the problem. This enabled units to build on each other's thoughts and successes rather than start from scratch. Once the "fix" was determined, the CAATs got busy with their second task: disseminating information on "what" and "how" to all tank units in the United Nations force. In a remarkably short period of time, the problem was solved throughout the area using a classic bit of in-the-field ingenuity (the semi-official term is *work-around*) involving duct tape and other materials at hand. In short, it was the sort of solution which Americans have long prided themselves on.

38 *Chapter Seven*

Figure 7   Take some duct tape and call me in the morning.

The actions of CALL ensured that all appropriate individuals and units were informed of the lesson. When everyone saw that implementing the improvement did, in fact, make it possible for tanks to operate, the lesson became institutionalized and behavior was changed—and ready for further improvement.

IN WAR AND IN PEACE

As is evident from the situation described in the previous section, an AAR is not just a peacetime tool. *A Leader's Guide to After-Action Reviews* states:

> *The AAR is one of the most effective techniques to use in a combat environment. An effective AAR takes little time, and leaders can conduct them almost anywhere consistent with unit security requirements. Conducting AARs helps*

overcome the steep learning curve that exists in a unit exposed to combat and helps the unit ensure that it does not repeat mistakes. It also helps them to sustain strengths. By integrating training into combat operations and using tools such as AARs, leaders dramatically increase their unit's chances for success on the battlefield.

The manual goes on to acknowledge somewhat dryly that AARs continue in combat "although limited time and proximity to the enemy may restrict the type and extent of training. Only training improves combat performance without imposing the stiff penalties combat inflicts on the untrained." The fact that AARs are now a vital part of how the army operates in combat zones should go a long way toward convincing hesitant executives that the AAR process has a place in the real world. If the object is to improve performance quickly, when better to make that effort than when an organization's future is literally at risk?

AARs alone, though, are not sufficient. The other organization in the example, CALL, is also a vital link in organizational learning. After an AAR identifies a problem and a solution, the information is sent to CALL to be added to information from other units, analyzed, and distributed as needed. It is a far cry from the extensive use of "desktop procedures" in military units during the Vietnam War. At that point, the only way to preserve institutional knowledge was to have a person write down exactly what steps he went through to perform the basics of the job held: sequences, people to contact, phone numbers, times and dates things were due, and so on. In the permanent or temporary absence of the primary job-holder, someone else could step in and immediately keep things moving.

DO WE KNOW THAT OR NOT?

Handling information correctly is always a bugaboo. General Sullivan argues that in the case of looking at an organization's external environment, a major problem can be summed up with "We don't know what we don't know," while, when looking inward, the analogous problem is, "We don't know what we *do* know." The knowledge is there. It is inside the organization. The challenge is finding ways to identify it and distribute it so that everyone can be informed. CALL was designed to meet that challenge for the army.

CALL, headquartered at Ft. Leavenworth, Kansas, has emphasized "quick lesson turnaround" since its inception in 1985 (see Figure 8). CALL personnel comb through reports from AARs and from coordination efforts such as

Figure 8 CALL anytime.

the Lesson Learned Integration (L2I) program. CALL looks for patterns, for what may be happening that causes a particular behavior and for systematic breakthroughs that can be identified.

One of the most noteworthy aspects of CALL is that it ensures that information flows up the chain of command as well as down. Changes in instructions on how things are to be done too frequently originate only at the top of an organization. Senior management or research and development gets an idea and pushes it down the organizational ladder to the people who have to change how they do things. With CALL in place, the army has set in motion a procedure whereby ideas originating at the lowest level (where, in corporate-speak, "the rubber meets the road") are also catalysts for change.

CALL ensures that the lessons identified in AARs or in any other way lead to changes in general behavior throughout the army whenever appropriate. Particularly in combat, when lessons are too often bought with blood, there is an urgent need to ensure that lessons identified lead to lessons learned as effectively as possible to make the sacrifice even begin to be worthwhile.

Janet Wray, Public Information Officer at Fort Leavenworth, Kansas, reports that, "In 2006, CALL placed dedicated military analysts in all TRADOC (Training and Doctrine Command) schools and centers and in selected corps and divisions. This is in addition to the existing observation detachments in Iraq, Afghanistan, and Kuwait, and in the combat training centers [in the United States]. Their purpose is to enhance rapid information sharing and facilitate integration of best practices and issue resolution across the Army."

SUCCESS AND FAILURE

CALL has helped redefine what the army used to call "failure." Many consultants and speakers try to force the word "opportunity" into their readers' and listeners' vocabularies in place of the word "problem"; CALL actually does something about it. The difference in how failure is perceived lies in the focus on task and process.

CALL not only looks at instances in which problems were encountered, it also spends a great deal of time studying successes. What may look at first to be "lucky" or the function of a singular personality usually turns out to be influenced greatly by identifiable—and, thus, repeatable—factors. This includes looking for successes in the midst of mediocrity, when one portion of an overall lackadaisical effort shines through. The factors that are studied by CALL in determining how to change organizational behavior are leadership, doctrine, training, organization, material and soldiers/people.

Besides reviewing the results of single AARs in isolated units or the build-upon-each-other's thoughts ad hoc collaboration of a group of units (such as with the tank filters in Saudi Arabia), CALL is able to look at a complicated set of interwoven events (such as a 100,000-man training exercise or a movement to a foreign country) and pick it apart to find not only the things that went awry, but also the things that went right, as both are potential sources of information on how to improve.

THE CALL EXPERIENCE

CALL considers itself to have three customers: the host unit with which it is working, follow-on units, and the army as a whole. The CALL staff exists both to collect information and to disseminate it, functioning as any level unit's two-way communications link to the army's central database and to the rest of the army. As a result, lessons learned anywhere in the army are now available throughout the force.

General Sullivan says that the CALL experience in the army suggests a six-step process, provided with paraphrased comments below:

1. *Targeting opportunity:* deciding what to learn from and where the biggest possibilities for improvement are located

2. *Collecting data:* an operation that must be kept as unambiguous as possible so that all participants will accept the data

3. *Creating knowledge:* some of the data will have to be collated and otherwise organized in order to convert the information into intelligence

4. *Distributing knowledge:* by both the *push strategy,* whereby personnel with the new knowledge go to particular locations to ensure the information is received and learned, and the *pull strategy,* whereby the information is made available to all appropriate individuals and units

5. *Short-term applications:* things that are relatively easy to diagnose and correct and may be of use to someone starting a similar operation in the short period of time

6. *Long-term applications:* information that addresses systemic issues and will help to shape future policies and strategies

A cautionary note: Lessons from CALL are a *beginning point for action.* They are not a straitjacket. The title of one typical publication from CALL, for example, is *Peace Operations Training Vignettes with Possible Solutions.* Once a plan is put into operation in the field, there likely will be changes. New experiences are themselves subject to an AAR and revisions are sent on to Ft. Leavenworth. CALL personnel look for new patterns and revise their advice accordingly.

IT WORKS!

As with anything, the proof is in the doing. When the U.S. troops were first sent into Haiti in 1994, the army unit—which had already benefited significantly from the AARs conducted by army troops in Somalia the previous year—conducted AARs after virtually every incident of any sort and sent in its results. CALL used that information as the starting point to develop training scenarios designed for army units slated to go to Haiti. After that second unit completed its tour, the commanding officer notified CALL that his troops had encountered twenty-three of the twenty-four training scenarios provided them. Thanks to their preparation, troops had a baseline for action rather than having to start their own learning curve from zero. What was the scenario that the units didn't have to face? A general rebel uprising.

CALL is, in short, the army's vehicle for ensuring that it can benefit from its own lessons, old and new. When the 1st Armored Division went into Bosnia in December, 1996, one of its first and most important tasks was to establish zones of separation (ZOS), by which the warring factions were to be separated physically. The ZOS concept had been spelled out in the Dayton Peace Accords, but no one had any specific idea on how to go about it. The need for haste made things more difficult.

The senior leaders of the force in the field asked CALL what information was available. A thorough search of the CALL-maintained database came up empty, so a member of the Actual Operations Branch of the Lessons Learned Division of CALL went to the library of the Command and

General Staff College, also located at Ft. Leavenworth, and discovered a document prepared by an armored cavalry regiment in Germany in the 1960s, at the height of the Cold War. The document spelled out how to establish and patrol borders between potentially hostile areas. The document's original intent was to define how to maintain the separation of West Germany from Iron Curtain countries, but the well-thought-out, basic ideas provided a wealth of information. The document was faxed to Bosnia and served as a wonderfully rich starting point for the command staff there, saving not only hundreds of hours of time-consuming work but also, no doubt, lives.

SUMMING UP

Colonel Lawrence H. Saul, former CALL director, described the role of CALL in these terms: "CALL collects, analyzes, disseminates, integrates, and archives Army and joint, interagency, and multinational observations, insights, and lessons (OIL) and tactics, techniques and procedures (TTP) to support the full spectrum of military operations of the United States and U.S. coalition partners and allies. CALL succeeds when soldiers and leaders survive because of what they learned today based on what happened yesterday and when OIL becomes integrated in training and doctrine development and military education."

IF YOU DON'T ALREADY DO IT, START NOW

Accumulating and disseminating knowledge is too important to leave to chance. There must be a specific person—or people—designated to ensure that information gathering takes place and that the data are treated as something of value. Responsibility must be assigned and repeatable procedures spelled out and agreed upon.

Gathering data, converting it to knowledge, and broadcasting the outcome must be the result of conscious effort; it cannot simply be assumed.

Until recently, corporate America had not been conspicuously successful in learning from past effort, although it might be argued that a slow-motion version of CALL existed when organizations were the source of lifetime employment. Then, someone working at the lowest levels knew with a high degree of certainty that his (or, only sometimes in those days, her) turn would come at being a boss. As a result, individuals noted lessons and filed them away as, "Things I am going to do differently when it is my turn to run the show." That corporate-memory-through-lifetime-employment approach is clearly not suited to today's economy.

The quality revolution, with its emphasis on imitating success, inspired a more proactive approach. In many major corporations, quality departments became clearing-houses for information handling and retrieval, often with dramatic results. At Paul Revere Insurance Group, whose main line of business was disability income, executives consulted the company's quality idea tracking program when it came time to develop a new insurance policy. They found a number of "orphan ideas"—ideas from field teams that the home office had considered impractical standing alone. Looked at all together, more than two hundred of these orphans were combined into a new disability income proposal. Companies that have data on call have a significant advantage over companies that do not.

8
A New Learning Cycle

One U.S. corporation beginning to experiment with an AAR-like tool for organizational learning is Harley-Davidson, maker of the classic American motorcycle. As members of the Society for Organizational Learning, Harley-Davidson executives became acquainted with officers of the U.S. Army, which is also a member. Their relationship led to Harley-Davidson's sending Tim Savino, Director of Development and Training, to Ft. Irwin. He witnessed portions of a war game, with particular emphasis on observing AARs conducted in the field, on a base roughly the size of the state of Rhode Island.

One of the challenges facing Harley-Davidson is that its company culture has always been action oriented, that is, it has long leaned toward what Tom Peteres identified (and praised) as a "Ready-Fire-Aim" approach in which the emphasis is on doing something, even if it's not the perfect thing to do. The premise is that doing something and then rapidly correcting it is far superior to doing nothing. Peter Senge, director of the Society for Organizational Learning, presents a slightly different perspective: "Slower is faster." Both approaches can be carried to extremes. To offset its bias, the Harley-Davidson executives held an offsite meeting in early 1998 with the objective of expanding its corporate culture to value reflection (see Figure 9).

48 *Chapter Eight*

Figure 9 All revved up and ready to reflect.

Reflection is a vital component of leadership and one that surfaces in virtually every biography or autobiography of those men and women who have earned reputations as leaders. Unfortunately, setting aside time for reflection is rare. Even a thirty-minute period of reflection is probably twenty-nine minutes and thirty seconds longer than is common, particularly at lower levels in an organization. Until organizations understand the benefits of reflection, the situation is not likely to change.

After his visit to Ft. Irwin, Savino concurred with Holland and Baird's assessment that an AAR "carves out a legitimate space for reflection" through a conscious assessment of what just happened. Harley-Davidson began its efforts at incorporating AAR-like procedures by asking its platform managers to conduct AARs after each development cycle for any project under their direction.

JUMP-START

The road for an AAR-like activity had been paved by an annual "Good News–Bad News" new product launch report that has been used at Harley-Davidson since the early 1990s. These reports are what the name implies: frank discussions of both the good and the not-so-good outcomes that took place while a product launch was in progress. A weakness of the Good News–Bad News reports has been that they occur at long intervals. Further complicating matters is the fact that there had been no standardized method established to respond to the information that is generated by the reports. While the frequency with which AARs are conducted in the Army is important and is itself something to be emulated, the impact of the AARs would be barely noticeable without the formalized efforts at follow-up action.

Happily, the initial reactions of the platform managers have been positive. Of course, more challenges await Harley-Davidson as it continues to harness the brainpower of all its employees to fend off both foreign and domestic competitors. One of the greatest challenges will be how to collect, organize, archive, and make available throughout the organization the lessons identified during its AARs. The goal, as Savino puts it, is to "make system changes before the next guy has to try to learn a lesson that somebody else has already learned."

9

Taking AARs International

"It's been a great marriage," said Director of Human Resources Kathy Brosmith, referring to the relationship between the army and a major division of Motorola, Inc., the Cellular Infrastructure Group (CIG). The relationship began in 1997. Motorola CIG was looking for a resource to enhance the group's personal training and leadership development curriculum. About-to-be-retired General Sullivan was wondering whether a training technique he used with his staff might be applicable in U.S. corporations. Once Sullivan and Brosmith connected, they agreed that their organizations could learn from each other, thus forming a firm foundation for their future alliance.

With the endorsement of senior CIG management, Brosmith initially set up a "Staff Ride" for the group's executive vice president and general manager and all of his direct reports. A second Staff Ride for a larger group of strategic planners followed. Each three-day Staff Ride visited three Civil War battlefields, Antietam, Gettysburg, and the Wilderness, where three retired army officers—military historian General Harold Nelson; Colonel Mike Harper, coauthor of *Hope Is Not a Method*; and General Sullivan—talked about the battles. In the evening, attendees took part in an AAR of the day's activities.

CONVERTING THE WARY

When announced, enthusiasm for planned visits was underwhelming. By the end of the first day, however, it became obvious that the battlefield experience provided a strong metaphor for the international marketplace: Time is compressed, the issue is survival, and outcomes define the future. Discussions in the AARs centered around personal relationships, organizational learning, and strategy. Participants identified a number of common issues, such as the press of technology (cannons versus rifle/analog versus digital), the difficulty of communicating intent over long distances (units on a battlefield/divisions of an international corporation), and the role of happenstance (Clara Barton and the Red Cross/CIG and its ability to spot a need).

It was a productive few days with long-range impact. The Staff Rides crystallized six leadership essentials subsequently published throughout CIG and forged a concrete plan for the future. As Brosmith summed up, "We spend time as a senior team looking at our mistakes or missed opportunities. We don't make time to examine why we succeeded. One of the things we learned from the army is that they do both. We need to do a better job of that." After watching an AAR, she was convinced that here was the vehicle for doing a better job.

The team realized that the military as a leadership model would be a tough sell to those unable to participate. To counter that, they arranged for a crew to film the Staff Ride on the battlefields and in the classroom. The result was a twenty-minute videotape designed not only to introduce the army and what military history could teach CIG about a leadership culture and strategy, but also to enable employees to see senior managers in a learning environment.

Before instituting Motorola CIG's own version of AARs, the next logical step was a trip to observe AARs in the field at Ft. Irwin. Participants were impressed by the openness and honesty, the sense of community coupled with the sense that "I am capable" demonstrated by the soldiers of all ranks at Ft. Irwin. That experience was the impetus for a small group of CIG personnel to establish a non-officially-funded pilot program. The idea was to pick a system installation and conduct an AAR of the project.

GIVING IT A TRY

The project chosen was the implementation of a system using new technology in a major Asian market. It was the first such installation in this market and would, it was hoped, lay the groundwork for similar installations in years to come. The project was first named Implementation Supremacy Review (ISR) and then, when it began to look as though it would take root, the Implementation Supremacy Process (ISP).

In some ways, Motorola CIG was uniquely prepared to introduce the use of AARs into its culture. Beginning with Robert Galvin, a past CEO of Motorola, the number-one rule at Motorola has been "constant respect for people." Values, seen as a history of shared beliefs, are important at Motorola, as is an emphasis on leadership development throughout the organization. The ground rules for AARs were in place.

CIG developed a half-day training program for part-time facilitators, a carefully chosen combination of process specialists from the quality department, subject matter experts, and a retired general who is a colleague of Sullivan's. The decision to include a military veteran who was not an employee of Motorola was made despite initial hesitation. He proved to be an excellent choice. Based on his previous experience with dozens (if not hundreds) of AARs, he was especially adept at knowing when to offer guidance to a discussion and when to sit back and let a conversation evolve until a learning point was developed.

Before launching the pilot, the critical questions were, "Would the employees support the process?" and "Would the organization support the process?" The majority of people who responded to a carefully crafted invitation letter and attended the ISR arrived skeptical but willing to listen. They left impressed. Shortly after the ISR, each participant received a four-page document listing the lessons learned. Among these lessons, CIG personnel decided to modify the ISR itself. They dropped the role of "historian/note-taker" in the back of the room and added the role of "facilitator/note-taker" in the front of the room so that what was recorded and summarized would be done with the concurrence and knowledge of the attendees.

ASSESSING THE RESULTS

Perhaps the surest sign of the success of this first Motorola AAR (staffed by a design team that obtained the necessary funding from departmental budgets) is the fact that the general manager is looking at future funding for what are now called ISP efforts. Within weeks after the completion of the first one, four more were scheduled for the year.

In the future, CIG hopes to steer people away from thinking of an ISP as a postmortem and demonstrate how ISPs contribute to active learning during a project. Lessons from ISPs are to be incorporated before the next ISP whenever possible. With a means in place for identifying lessons, a more formal approach to storing and retrieving data will be developed in the future.

Although the large-scale formal AAR may become an official part of how Motorola CIG goes about its business, small-scale, unit-level AARs remain in the unofficial mode. But Baldrige-winner Motorola has a track record of recognizing good ideas and incorporating them into its everyday procedures. So the use of AARs at all levels to investigate a variety of activities followed by efforts to identify and institutionalize lessons may become part of the Motorola way of doing things.

10
Exploring the Depths of Knowledge

Amoco's exploration and production sector methodically assesses the size and risk of the corporation's drilling prospects worldwide, using a full-time, ten-member Prospect Quality Team (PQT). When we visited Ft. Irwin in 1997, Don Baldwin, an Amoco vice president, noted marked similarities between the PQT process and the Army's AAR/CALL process. Amoco executives now look to the army for ideas that might be useful in their own processes.

The Amoco process is given credit for a near-phenomenal bottom-line impact. In 1990, Amoco experienced success in only 10 percent of its sixty drilling attempts, and in 1991, the success rate was 11 percent (nine successes in eighty attempts). Since initiation of the PQT process, the success rate has increased dramatically. In 1997, after reviewing more than three hundred prospective drilling sites, thirty-two were attempted and fifteen were successes—a success rate of 46.9 percent. The international average for successful exploration drilling operations is in the 20 to 25 percent range, with a success percentage of approximately 35 percent considered in the industry to be world class. In addition, between 1990 and 1995, the pre-drill resource estimates as a percentage of actual discovered portfolio resources improved from 20 percent to 90 percent. In other words, not only do they know better where to drill, they also know better what to expect when they do drill.

SUCCESS FROM THE GROUND DOWN

As may be expected in any new effort that forces people to change their approach to how they work, the PQT process was not immediately greeted as an answer to prayer. In fact, the members of the PQT were initially called the RISK Police, the derisive name drawn in part from the name of the Monte Carlo computer program that compiles the riskiness of the prospect in the computer-assisted assessment process.

Now, after several years of "persistence, patience, and fortitude" plus undeniable success, assignment to the PQT is seen in the organization as a prestigious accomplishment. Gary Citron, a member of the PQT and a geoscientist by training, recently expressed regret that his tour of duty was drawing to a close. He had a hard time imagining another job in the company that would put him so close to all of the exciting action, especially with the company's escalating rate of success.

Careful adherence to all three steps of the 3-I learning cycle makes Amoco's efforts successful. An organization that admits its efforts were previously anecdote-driven is now data driven. Better yet, Amoco doesn't just gather ideas or lessons, it makes all information available to all appropriate people and units in the company, and it is active in ensuring that the information is accessed and used. In other words, the PQT functions both as the gatherers of information and as the custodians of a database that is made available to everyone in the company as soon as possible. Like CALL, the PQT uses both the pull strategy and the push strategy to ensure that the needed information reaches the right hands and minds.

Here's how it works: The cycle begins with a pre-drill assessment during which PQT personnel work with exploration personnel to apply to the proposed project lessons from previous efforts. This formal presentation of information reminds participants that information accumulated and organized from previous drilling operations is available on a database at any time. Sometimes even the best of executives and workers need to be reminded about the data within their reach.

In addition to hard data recorded in thirteen categories, such as "reservoir rock thickness," "porosity," and "gas/oil ratio," decisions reached during the pre-drill discussions are routinely recorded so that insights can be captured and, if appropriate, made a part of future considerations. The corporation concedes that incorporating archival information in the conversation and reaching consensus is often time consuming, but it believes that the investment has proven its worth (see Figure 10). Case studies and points of

Figure 10 Hit a gusher!

data available virtually ensure that it is always possible to locate one or more parallel situations.

After the drilling operation has either succeeded or failed, the PQT leads a post-appraisal of the effort. Post-appraisals are conducted even of those drilling efforts in which Amoco has had initial interest but ultimately did not follow through—whether Amoco lost out in the bidding for the drilling site or decided that the site wasn't worth pursuing.

The stated objectives of the Amoco post-appraisal are:

1. Understand the exploratory risks
2. Focus the application of our best technology
3. Drive exploration research and technology strategy
4. Share the lessons learned across the organization and apply these lessons to future prospects
5. Calibrate our RISK system

During the post-appraisal effort, procedural ideas and technical data are archived for ongoing analysis and use. Frequent revisiting of the database and addition of new information are the keys to what Amoco refers to as "calibrating the process." Continual efforts to enrich the database have driven the spectacular rate of improvement of its efforts.

WE STRUCK A GUSHER!

The dramatic impact of the PQT efforts on the company's bottom line—to say nothing of the savings in frustration and wear and tear on people and equipment when 80-90 percent of drilling attempts fail—has ensured the third "I," institutionalization. No one even considers beginning a project without the PQT's input. Signs of the institutionalization of the process include executives volunteering to join the PQT unit when vacancies appear and other departments of Amoco beginning to adapt the PQT approach to their own procedures. Baldwin's advice incorporates the three I's for PQT-wanna-bes: Begin by investigating the situation, identify and archive information, and make sure information is used as a basis for future decisions.

The success of the PQT builds credibility with customers. Members of the PQT find themselves giving presentations, describing to their audiences how they can deliver what they say they will deliver with a higher rate of success than any competitor. This "power of prediction" positions them favorably in the race for potential partners and customers.

Amoco's summation of the impact of the PQT process on its exploration business is succinct: Amoco is now in the business of "creating value." It does this by returning to the corporation results of far greater value than the cost of the PQT and the exploration efforts combined.

11
Choosing Success

A lawsuit is a powerful testimonial to the importance of knowledge to an organization. As reported in the January 12, 1998, issue of *Business Week*, Viacom, Inc., went to court to stop Rich Cronin from accepting a job with News Corporation, a Viacom competitor. Although other issues no doubt were at play, the basis of Viacom's stated complaint was twofold: not only would Cronin's departure mean a decrease in the information available to Viacom, but it would mean an increase in the knowledge base of a competitor.

It is ironic that although some organizations go to great lengths to protect knowledge, many more squander it. Organizations routinely fail to formalize and, when appropriate, institutionalize what individuals know—mostly because it is hard work to ensure that knowledge is recorded and becomes part of a commonly held database. Handling information wisely is not rocket science. An investigate-identify-institutionalize cycle for organizational learning enables any organization to ensure that, in addition to benefiting in the short term from the talents of the individuals on the payroll, long-term benefits accrue: core competency, continuous improvement, leadership skills, and bottom-line profits.

INVESTIGATE, IDENTIFY, INSTITUTIONALIZE

The major benefit of a 3-I learning cycle is its synergistic effect (see Figure 11). Ideas build on one another, to include second-generation and third-generation ideas on the same topic. Organizations need both mechanics and encouragement to improve on their own improvements. With the AAR process backed up by CALL, an army unit located on the East Coast of the United States can initiate an improvement, the idea can subsequently be improved by a unit stationed in Germany, and a unit in California can add a further refinement. All three changes benefit units throughout the army, but the second might not have been possible without the first, and the third might never have been thought of without the first two.

Any organization can use a 3-I learning cycle to its advantage. Size is no barrier. Large organizations have the

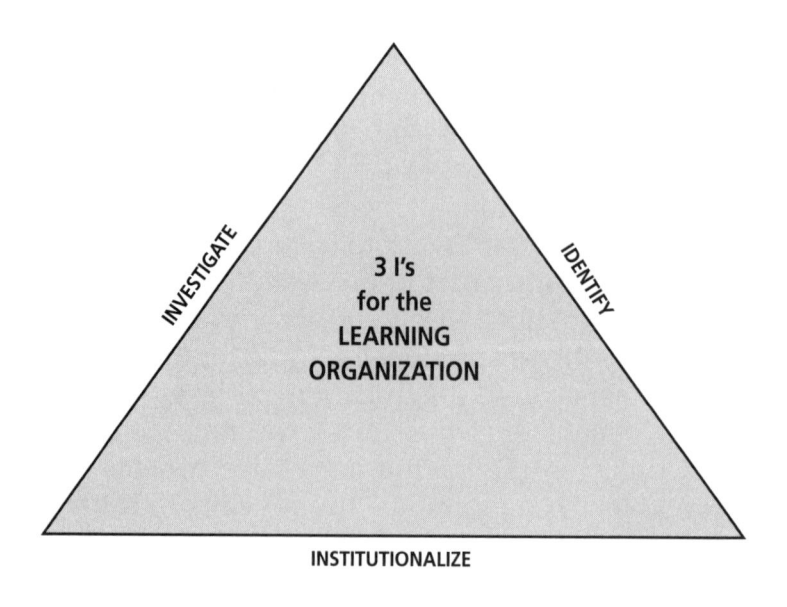

Figure 11 The three "I" words.

luxury of being able to assign a number of people to full-time jobs to facilitate organizational learning. The army, with its approximately 480,000 active-duty personnel, an organization about the size of Chrysler Corporation, has assigned a full-time staff of fourteen active-duty military and thirty-four civilians to CALL at Ft. Leavenworth. CALL can also call on the services of temporary CAAT teams such as the one used on the tank filter problem in Saudi Arabia, composed of active-duty military personnel on temporary duty. By mid-2007, CALL had almost 200 active-duty military, civilian, and contractor personnel located throughout the continental United States, Germany, Kuwait, Iraq, and Afghanistan.

Small organizations may have trouble developing a person or team that understands the principles well enough to devise a pragmatic set of mechanics for the 3-I process while continuing to perform regular jobs. Then again, the 3-I team in a large organization faces the daunting task of coordinating information throughout a number of units, some of them likely to be geographically distant, while a part-time 3-I person in a small organization will be able to speak personally with virtually anyone on the payroll.

No matter what the size, organizations without a well-conceived plan for investigating what is going on, identifying successes and failures, and ensuring that improvements become part of the "way things are done around here" are courting the worst kind of failure. In the words of former Army Chief of Staff General Gordon Sullivan, "The only real failure is the failure to learn."

References

1. Holland, Phillip and Lloyd Baird. "Facilitating Team Learning, the After-Action Review." (Unpublished paper.)
2. Stevens, Elizabeth Lesly. "Caught: a job-hunter. Penalty: house arrest." *Business Week.* January 12, 1998, p. 44.
3. Sullivan, Gordon R. and Michael V. Harper. *Hope Is Not a Method.* New York, NY: Broadway Books, 1997, pp. 189-210.
4. U.S. Army. *After-Action Review Training Support Package/Lesson Guide.* Ft. Irwin, CA: U.S. Army, 1998.
5. U.S. Army. *Cadet Command Regulations 145-3, TRADOC.* Ft. Monroe, VA: U.S. Army, p. H-1.
6. U.S. Army. *After-Action Review (AAR) Guide for the Army Training Battle Simulation System (ARTBASS).* Systems Research Laboratory, Ft. Leavenworth, KS, 1986.
7. U.S. Army. *A Leader's Guide to After-Action Reviews (TC 25-20).* Washington, DC, 1993.
8. U.S. Army. *National Training Center After-Action Review Guidebook (Research Product 83-11).* Monterey, CA: U.S. Army Research Institute for the Behavioral and Social Sciences, 1982.
9. Wray, Janet. Email dated April 10, 2007
10. U.S. Army. *Doctrine for Army Special Operations Forces (FM 100-25).* Fort Bragg, North Carolina, 1991

Further Reading

Sullivan, Gordon R. and Michael V. Harper. *Hope Is Not a Method.* New York, NY: Broadway Books, 1997.

Townsend, Patrick L., and Joan E. Gebhardt. *The Executive Guide to Understanding and Implementing Employee Engagement Programs.* Milwaukee, WI: ASQ Quality Press, 2007.

Townsend, Patrick L., and Joan E. Gebhardt. *Five-Star Leadership: The Art and Strategy of Creating Leaders at Every Level.* New York, NY: Wiley & Sons, 1997.

Townsend, Patrick L., and Joan E. Gebhardt. *Quality in Action: 93 Lessons in Leadership, Participation and Measurement.* New York, NY: Wiley & Sons, 1992.

Townsend, Patrick L., and Joan E. Gebhardt. *Quality Makes Money.* Milwaukee, WI: ASQ Quality Press, 2006.

Townsend, Patrick L., and Joan E. Gebhardt. *Recognition, Gratitude, & Celebration.* Milwaukee, WI: ASQ Quality Press, 2008.

U.S. Army. *A Leader's Guide to After-Action Reviews (TC 25-20).* Washington, DC: U.S. Army 1993.

Index

A

A Leader's Guide to After-Action Reviews
 on format for (sequence of events), 26–27, 30
 philosophy, 25
 on rules for Observer Controller, 19–20
 on the use of statistics, 28
AAR Guidebook
 on 'how can we do better?,' 15
 on Observer Controller's role, 20
 on the value of data, 28–29
after-action review (AAR)
 Amoco Oil Company, 55-59
 benefits of, 36
 from a civilian perspective, 33–36
 compared to traditional military briefings, 15
 defined, 4–5, 9
 emphasis on future behavior, 29, 34–35, 52
 format for (sequence of events), 26–27
 Harley-Davidson Motor Company, 47–49
 key points, 26
 and leadership skills, 11–12
 and link to quality, 15–16
 Motorola Cellular Infrastructure Group (CIG), 51, 53–59

 Observer Controller role in, 17-22, 28
 optimal conditions for, 14
 and organizational context, 19
 parallels in the business world, 11–12
 philosophy of, 25
 pitfalls, 18
 purposes of, 9
 success and failures, 25–26, 42
 and time context, 31
 training centers for, 31–32
 understanding the mission, 27–28
 and U.S. army's chain of learning, 9
Allaire, Paul, 15
Amoco Oil Company, 3, 55-59
Army War College, Strategic Studies Institute, 4

B

Baird, Lloyd, 36
 "Facilitating Team Learning: The After-Action Review," 34–35
Baldrige Award criteria, 4, 33-36
Baldwin, Don, 55
behavior, predictability of, 3
blame and punishment, avoiding, 25–26, 28
Bosnia, and after-action review, 44
breakthrough improvement, 1–2

Brosmith, Kathy, 51
Brumel, Valery, 1
Business Outreach Program, Army War College, 4
business world
 and after-action reviews, 11–12, 33–36, 52–53
 changing role of senior managers, 12–13
  Society for Organizational Learning, 4, 47
  staff meetings vs. quality team meetings, 15–16

C

CAAT. *See* Collection and Analysis Teams
CALL. *See* Center for Army Lessons Learned
Cellular Infrastructure Group (CIG), Motorola's, 51, 53–59
Center for Army Lessons Learned (CALL)
 and chain of command, 41
 follow-on units, 42–43
 host units, 42–43
 and organizational learning, 39
 personnel distribution, 63
 quick lesson turnaround, 40–41
 role of staff, 42–43
 three customers of, 42–43
 U.S. tank units and, 37–39
chain of learning, U.S. army's, 9
Citron, Gary, 56
cohesion through learning, 14–15
Cold War documents and after-action review, 44–45
Collection and Analysis Teams (CAAT), 37–38, 63
combat environments, after-action review in, 38–39
Combat Maneuver Training Center (Hohenfels, Germany), 31–32
communications, importance of open, 13

continual improvement, 29
corporate memory, 13-15, 39, 46
corporate world. *See* business world
Cronin, Rich, 61

D-E

data
 importance of, 28, 44–46, 58
 privacy of military, 31–32
Dayton Peace Accords, 44
discouragement, risk of, 19–20

F

"Facilitating Team Learning: The After-Action Review" (Holland and Baird), 34–35
failure and success, learning from, 3, 7–8, 25–26, 42
follow-on units (of CALL), 42–43
Ford Motor Company, 15
formal *vs.* informal after-action reviews, 30–31
Fosbury Flop, 1–2
future behavior, emphasis on, 29, 34-35, 52

G

GE (General Electric), 3, 12–13
Good News–Bad News reports, 49
ground truth, 28

H

Haiti, and after-action review, 44
Harley-Davidson Motor Company, 3, 47–49
Harper, Mike, 51
Holland, Philip, 34–35, 36
 "Facilitating Team Learning: The After-Action Review," 34–35
hop of hope *vs.* leap of faith, 16
host units (of CALL), 42–43

I

ideas, second- and third-generation, 62
"if it ain't broke, don't fix it," 15
Implementation Supremacy Process (ISP), 53–54
incremental improvement, 2
individual good *vs.* the organization, 13
informal *vs.* formal after-action reviews, 30–31
institutional memory, 3, 13–15, 39, 46
institutionalized falsification of data, 28
investigate-identify-institutionalize cycle. *See* 3-I approach to learning

J

Joint Readiness Training Center (Ft. Polk, Louisiana), 31–32

K

knowledge is power, 13

L

L. L. Bean, 4
leadership, 7–8, 11–12, 16
leadership model, military as, 52
leap of faith vs. hop of hope, 16
learning cycle. *See* 3-I approach to learning
Lesson Learned Integration program (L2I), 41

M

measurement, importance of, 28, 29
military
  altruistic mission of, 13
  as leadership model, 52
mission, importance of articulating, 27–28
Motorola Cellular Infrastructure Group (CIG), 3, 51, 53–59

N

Nelson, Harold, 51
no fault, no foul, 31–32
"no hurt feelings," 7–8, 12, 20

O

Observer Controller (OC), 17-22, 28
OIL (observations, insights, and lessons), 45
Olympic high jump records, 1–2
openness of exchange, importance of, 12
OPFOR (opposing force), 26
organizational memory, 13-15, 39, 46
"orphan ideas," 46

P

Paul Revere Insurance Group, 5–6, 46
Peters, Tom, 47
polite disputation, importance of, 12
Prospect Quality Team process (PQT), 55–59
punishment and blame, avoiding, 25–26, 28

Q

quality movement
  after-action reviews and, 15–16, 33–36
  and proactive approach to learning, 46
  senior leadership exercises for, 27
  and U.S. army parallels, 5
quality team meetings vs. staff meetings, 15–16
quick lesson turnaround, 40–41

R

ready-aim-fire approach to action, 47
reflection, value of, 48
Reid, Aubrey K., Jr., 5–6
respect, importance of, 20–21
RISK Police, 56

S

Saul, Lawrence H., 45
Savino, Tim, 47, 48, 49
second-generation ideas, 62
Senge, Peter, 47
senior management, role of, 12-13, 31
sharing information, importance of, 13
slower is faster approach to action, 47
Society for Organizational Learning, 4, 47
Somalia, and after-action review, 44
staff meetings vs. quality team meetings, 15–16
Staff Rides and Civil War battlefields, 51, 52–53
statistics, appropriate use of, 28
Strategic Studies Institute, Army War College, 4
success and failure, learning from, 3, 7-8, 25–26, 42
Sullivan, Gordon H.
   and after-action reviews, 10, 23
   on failure, 63
   on handling information, 40–41
   Hope is Not a Method, 10, 23
   on importance of tact and respect, 22
   and Motorola Cellular Infrastructure Group (CIG), 51
   on six-step CALL process, 43

T-U

tact, importance of, 20, 21–22
tank units and after-action reviews, 37–39
team learning, 34–35
third-generation ideas, 62
Thomas, John, 1
3-I approach to learning, 62
   Amoco Oil and, 56–59
   Baldrige Award and, 4
   benchmarking, 3–4
   major benefit of, 62
   in small and large organizations, 63
time horizons and after-action review (AAR), 35, 36
TRADOC (Training and Doctrine Command), 41
TTP (tactics, techniques, and procedures), 26, 45

V

valid criticism, withholding, 12
Viacom, Inc., 61
Vietnam War and after-action reviews, 9, 11

W

Wallace, William S., 17
work-arounds, 37–39
Wray, Janet, 41

X-Y

Xerox Corporation, 4

Z

zones of separation, 44

About the Authors

Pat Townsend and Joan Gebhardt both grew up as military dependents and Townsend spent 20 years in the Marine Corps. They drew on that experience for both this book and an earlier book, *Five-Star Leadership: The Art and Strategy of Creating Leaders at Every Level.* Townsend is a keynote speaker and together they conduct seminars on leadership and on the definition and implementation of continual improvement processes.

In addition to having more than 400 articles published, Townsend and Gebhardt have written seven other books on quality, leadership, and recognition.

They can be reached at authors@asq.org.